This book belongs to

_____

D1219506

This book is dedicated to parents, educators, and counselors everywhere. We have the most important job nurturing the next generation.

Ninja Life Hacks™

Emotionally Ninja Intelligent

By Mary Nhin

Pictures by
Jelena Stupar

When I saw that Lonely Ninja was looking sad, I asked...

I haven't always been emotionally intelligent.

Once upon a time, I really could get quite frustrated with not only my emotions, but other people's emotions, too.

When I got impatient with my brother, I would bark orders at him.

During school, if someone didn't get invited to a party, I could be quite insensitive...

If I had trouble reading some difficult words, I would become frustrated and give up.

As fate would have it, things changed when Zen Ninja introduced me to an exercise that would change my life forever.

The Emotion N.A.M.E. Game

MOOD METER

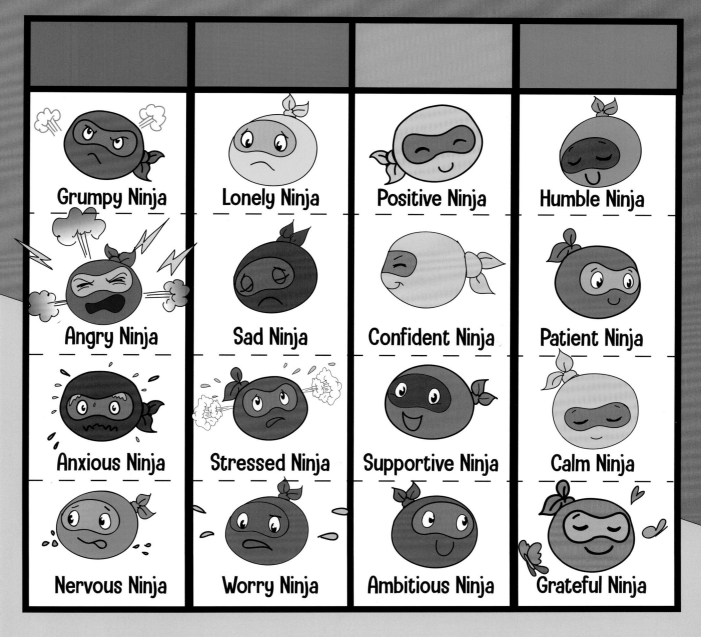

ANGRY

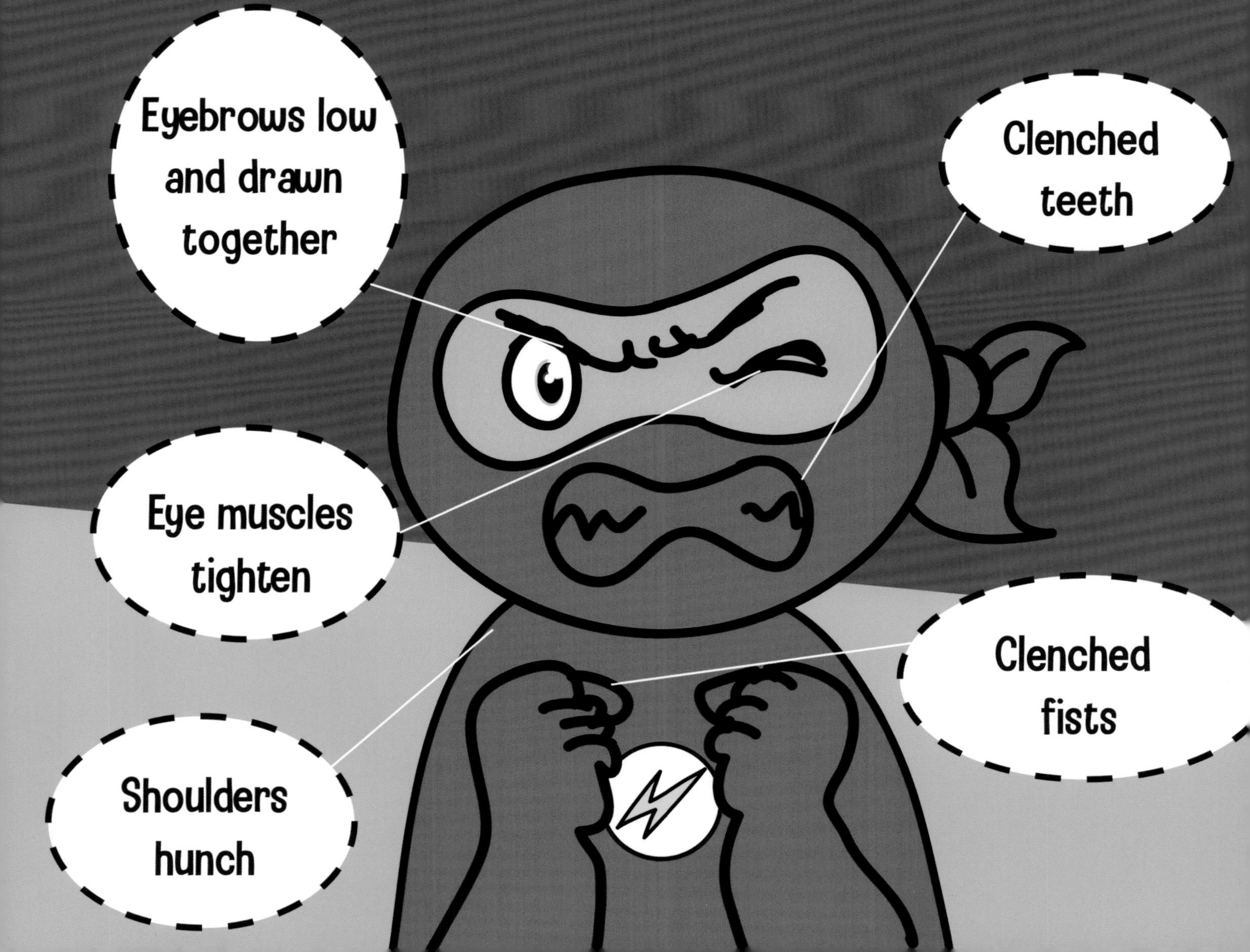
Eyebrows low and drawn together
Clenched teeth
Eye muscles tighten
Clenched fists
Shoulders hunch

Next, accept your emotion.

I am feeling

_____.

Then, manage your emotion.

Using the Emotion N. A. M. E. could be your secret weapon for becoming emotionally intelligent.

Visit us at NinjaLifeHacks.tv for fun, free printables.

@marynhin   @GrowGrit
#NinjaLifeHacks

Mary Nhin   Ninja Life Hacks

Ninja Life Hacks